D1264912

BODIES

Boris

VALLEJO

HIS PHOTOGRAPHIC ART

BODIES

BORIS
VALLEJO
HIS PHOTOGRAPHIC ART

THUNDER'S MOUTH PRESS
NEW YORK

Published in the United States by
Thunder's Mouth Press
632 Broadway, Seventh Floor
New York, New York 10012

First published by Dragon's World Ltd 1994

First Thunder's Mouth Press edtion 1996

© Dragon's World Ltd 1994
© Text: Boris Vallejo 1994
© Photographs: Boris Vallejo 1994

No part of this book may be reproduced or transmitted in any
form or by any means, electronic or mechanical, including
photocopy, recording, or any information storage and
retrieval system, without permission from the publisher, except
by a reviewer who may quote brief passages in a review.
All rights reserved

Library of Congress Catalog Number: 96-60078

ISBN 1-56025-126-3

Editor: Julie Davis
DTP Manager: Keith Bambury
Art Director: John Strange

Printed in Spain

**Distributed by
Publishers Group West
4065 Hollis Street
Emeryville, CA 94608**

INTRODUCTION

I got involved in photography in a rather indirect way. I am primarily an artist. I do fantasy work but I always use models for my paintings. The old masters used to make the models pose for them for hours, days and even weeks. I don't work that way. I prefer to take photographs of the models and then I work from the photographs.

Many years ago, at the beginning of my career as an illustrator, I used to work with a professional photographer in New York city. He would take the pictures for me. I would be there to direct the models and to tell the photographer what I needed, but he was in charge of the technical aspects of taking the photographs.

Gradually, I grew more and more interested in taking the photographs myself. I thought it would be easier, faster and more convenient if I could. So I started buying cameras, lights and other equipment and set up the basement of the house to serve as a studio. I didn't know much about the whole thing, but I got hooked on photography. I started reading as much as I could about it and, little by little, I started to progress.

Of course, my eye for composition and so on was already well developed because of my involvement with art, and this came very, very naturally. I used to think of interesting poses, good lighting and good composition. (I should say relatively good – I don't want to be too presumptuous.) The technical aspect was a little more difficult to get into. I wasn't too sure what exposure to give to the photographs, how strong the lighting should be or how to set the cameras.

I got hold of a Hasselblad camera which is about the best camera one can get – it's the Rolls Royce of cameras. I was lucky enough to be able to afford to buy one of these cameras and I started playing around with it. I had the

advantage of having access to a lot of really good models with terrific bodies. I was always interested – not only interested but also involved – in body building and I go to the gym frequently. I was also involved in judging professional body building contests and I was in touch with a lot of really good body builders with outstanding bodies.

People frequently ask me, when they see my paintings and the people I paint, if there really are people like that, if they really exist. A lot of people, of course, are not familiar with the super bodies of body builders. These people dedicate their lives to building their bodies. They are like musicians practising their instruments day after day, for years and years. They are very disciplined and work their bodies hard in the pursuit of excellence. People like that really do exist and this book is the proof of that.

One of the things that I emphasize to body builders when I work with them is that I do not want them to strike classic body building poses. I don't want them to be self-conscious about their muscles. I just want them to move around and do whatever comes naturally. I try to have a basic idea of what direction to go with the photographic session, especially if I am working with someone who has no experience as a model. Once I get an idea I can explain the concept to the model. I then let them move around and do different things. I may change the concept completely when I see what positions are more appropriate for the person.

If I work with someone with a lot of experience as a model, I let them do their own thing. I don't even suggest anything unless I see something happening as they are doing it. Since they have the experience, I like to capture the personality of the model. I feel that if they move in a certain way it's because that's the way they feel. They know how to display their bodies to best advantage. I am really fascinated by the human body. I don't have much interest in landscape, still life or portrait photography, but what really catches my attention is the human body. I really love human bodies – I think they are just so beautiful. I don't think I could ever get tired of working with the human body.

When working with body builders, it is sometimes very difficult to try to make them understand that I don't need them in what is called contest shape. Body builders get into contest shape about one week or so before a contest. At that point the body is at its most depleted of fat and water and the muscles are much better delineated. That takes a lot of dieting and control of what they eat.

I try to avoid that kind of condition because although it looks very good on stage for competition, I prefer to see the body looking fuller and rounder. I think the body is more sensual – and I am not just talking about women, I am talking about men too – if it looks rounder and not so super-defined and super-vascular. So that's one thing I really like to emphasize in my photography.

These people are the best of the best, but not all of them are body builders. I would say that probably 60 per cent are body builders and maybe 40 per cent are not – well, maybe 30 per cent – but even among those that are not body builders, they are people with beautiful bodies. And that is still my approach to the photography. It is not the approach of glamour photography. I do not do glamour *per se*. I like to present the body as naturally as I can. I don't touch up the photographs. I don't set up lights specifically to blur things or to minimise blemishes, scars or, what could be considered, imperfections. I think these people are beautiful as they are. I don't care if they have marks on their bodies.

I want people to see what a beautiful body looks like as a real person. I don't want to give the impression that these people are marble or bronze statues or anything like that. They are outstanding as they are. I don't have to change or modify anything to make them look better. I am certainly not interested in pin-up photography. I don't want to convey that kind of a message. I just love the human body and I would like to present it as a beautiful thing under the most natural conditions.

Every now and then I use a filter. Not usually when I take photographs, but when I print them. I use filters not to cover any imperfections in the body, but to create a mood and then only sparingly. I always print my own photographs. I don't like to ask someone else to do this and I don't give my negatives to a lab. I've printed all the photographs in this book. Purists may find fault with what I do, but that's the way I like to do it. It's just me, I give 100 per cent to everything I do.

There is a notable predominance of women in the book. I have a preference for the female body – a sexual preference, but I have to admit that when I'm taking pictures, the sexual aspect does not come into my mind and I enjoy taking pictures of men just as much as of women. When I'm working I can't really allow myself to have any sexual feelings. I'm just too busy working with the lights and shapes and paying attention to what I am doing. In that sense, it is just as challenging and enjoyable working with men as it is with women. I have included fewer men in the book because I find male body builders are not as graceful as women. Their bodies are great, but the men seem to be more self-conscious about their muscles. It's hard to find models who not only have amazing development but are also able to present their bodies in a graceful manner.

I use very few props in my photography. Every now and then I may use swords or knives as props. Frequently ropes appear in my photographs, but I really prefer to work just with bodies; over-use of props can be gimmicky. Doing without props simply makes it more challenging to find new ways to present the body and make it look exciting and different. So I change the lights, change the poses, and use different people to try to create new moods with as little use of props as possible.

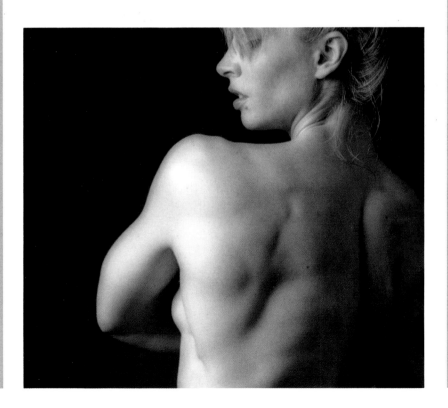

I don't take portrait photographs. Most of the time the face is away from the camera. I don't look for eye contact with the camera at all. I feel that makes the whole thing a little bit too suggestive, too much like a pin-up, and I try to stay away from that. Only occasionally do I show the face of the model; I think keeping the person incognito gives more attention to the body itself.

Another important aspect of my photography is my studio. I still have a very small studio with a low ceiling. I have moved from the house where I first took up photography, but I still work in the basement. The ceiling is very low, probably only about $7^1/_2$ feet high ($2^1/_2$ metres), and I'm very limited in terms of how much I can play with the light. Nevertheless, I try to be as creative as I can with it. There are many ways that one can work around it. My daughter, Maya, is a professional photographer and I get a lot of tips from her on the technical aspects of photography. My son, Dorian, is an illustrator and it's wonderful to have these two major interests in common with them. I get a lot of tips from my daughter and when I was complaining about having a small studio she said to me, 'When you are good you can shoot in a shoe box and still take good photographs'. I really like that a lot, I think it says a lot for not complaining about everything, but just making the best of what you have.

How do I choose a model? Obviously the most important thing I look for is a good body. A body with interesting contrast in terms of shapes. Small joints, round bellies of the muscles, a really exciting looking body to begin with and then, of course, the ability to convey a mood, to move, and be fluid. Sometimes you can get someone who looks outstanding but they may be a little rigid in front of the camera. At other times you may get someone who is not quite as well developed, but they move with grace and present their bodies at the best angles, so the photographs are really outstanding. On occasion, you can spend two hours taking photographs and shoot dozens of pictures and not get one right. Sometimes you have a session where everything goes right and works perfectly.

I frequently work with my wife, Julie. She is a body builder and she has one of the most perfect bodies that I have seen in my life — and I've seen a lot of bodies. She is not only a beautiful woman with a beautiful body, but she is also an exquisite model. It's really great to have the advantage of having someone at home you can spend time working with. She is also an experienced artist in her own right and I think that contributes a lot to her understanding of modelling. About a third of the pictures in this book are of my wife, Julie.

Boris W Vallejo

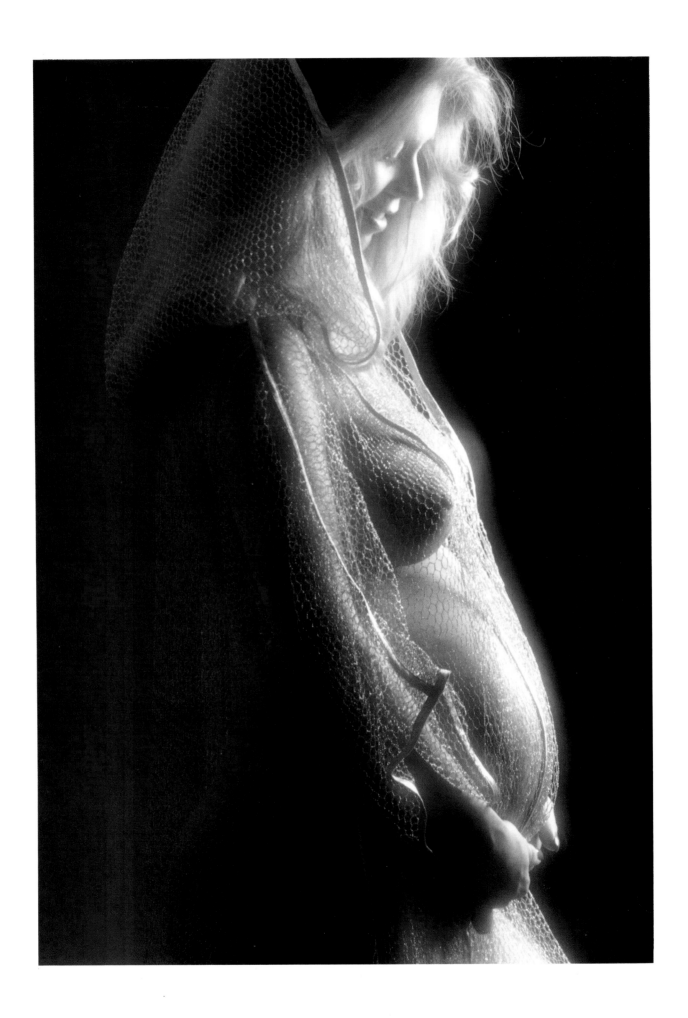

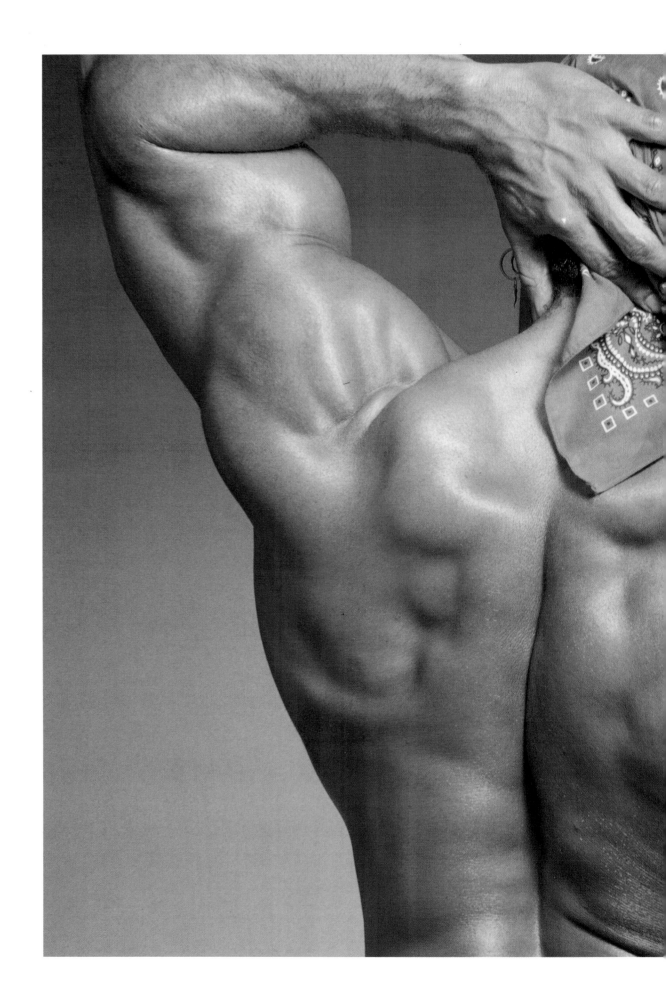

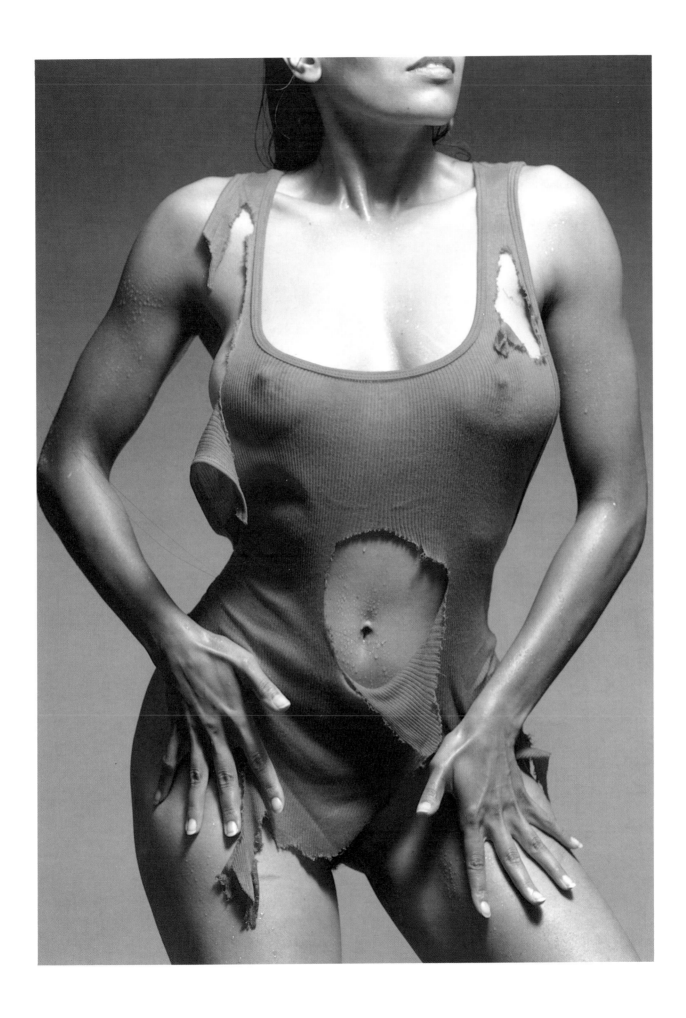

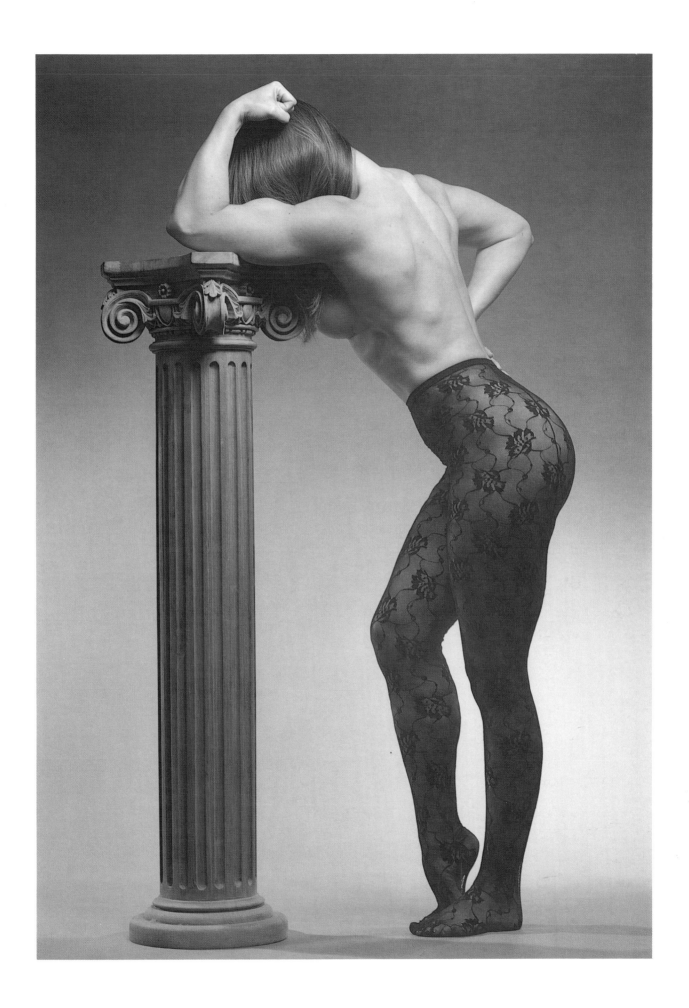